...ngest established
...wn travel brands,
experts in travel.

...han 135 years our
...ocked the secrets
...round the world,
...ellers a wealth of
experience and a passion for travel.

**Rely on Thomas Cook as your
travelling companion on your next trip
and benefit from our unique heritage.**

Thomas Cook **pocket** guides

DURHAM

Thomas
Cook

Written by Paul Shawcross

Published by Thomas Cook Publishing

A division of Thomas Cook Tour Operations Limited
Company registration no. 3772199 England
The Thomas Cook Business Park, Unit 9, Coningsby Road,
Peterborough PE3 8SB, United Kingdom
Email: books@thomascook.com, Tel: +44 (0) 1733 416477
www.thomascookpublishing.com

Produced by Cambridge Publishing Management Limited
Burr Elm Court, Main Street, Caldecote CB23 7NU
www.cambridgepm.co.uk

ISBN: 978-1-84848-492-4

First edition © 2011 Thomas Cook Publishing
Text © Thomas Cook Publishing
Cartography supplied by Redmoor Design, Tavistock, Devon
Map data © OpenStreetMap contributors CC-BY-SA, www.openstreetmap.org,
www.creativecommons.org

Series Editor: Karen Beaulah
Production/DTP: Steven Collins

Printed and bound in Spain by GraphyCems

Cover photography © Paul Walters/Thomas Cook Publishing

CONTENTS

SYMBOLS KEY

The following symbols are used throughout this book:

ⓐ address **ⓣ** telephone **ⓦ** website address **ⓔ** email
ⓛ opening times **ⓝ** public transport connections **ⓘ** important

The following symbols are used on the maps:

𝒊 information office			point of interest
✈ airport		◯	city
➕ hospital		◯	large town
🛡 police station		○	small town
🚌 bus station		=	motorway
🚃 railway station		—	main road
Ⓣ tram			minor road
✝ cathedral		—	railway
✉ post office		🛍	shopping
❶ numbers denote featured cafés, restaurants & venues			

PRICE CATEGORIES

Restaurant ratings in this book are based on the average
price of a three-course dinner without drinks.
£ under £15   **££** £15–40   **£££** over £40
Accommodation ratings are based on the average price of
a double room per night, including breakfast.
£ under £60   **££** £60–100   **£££** over £100

◗ *Durham Cathedral cloister*

INTRODUCING
Durham

Introduction

Durham is one of England's smaller cities; situated in the heart of the northeastern county with which it shares a name. Perched high on a peninsula formed by a tight bend in the river Wear, Durham's splendid cathedral and castle stand majestically over the rest of the city. It is a magnificent sight unequalled anywhere in the UK and, some would argue, in all of Northern Europe. Sir Nikolaus Pevsner, the great 20th-century art and architecture historian, wrote of it: 'Durham is one of the great experiences of Europe. The group of cathedral, castle and monastery on the rock can only be compared to Avignon and Prague.' In 2007, it was voted Condé Nast Traveller's 'Favourite UK City' by its readers and has been described by the renowned travel writer Bill Bryson as a 'perfect little city', which 'I fell in love with in a serious way'.

A university city since 1832 and a thriving commercial centre serving its many surrounding villages, Durham receives visitors from all over the world. Many are attracted by the UNESCO World Heritage Site of the cathedral and castle, as well as by the medieval streets and bridges and the relaxed, friendly and youthful ambience contributed to by the city's large student population.

Today, it is difficult to imagine the Durham of the 19th and 20th centuries: the centre of a vast coal-mining area that stretched up into neighbouring Northumberland. Indeed, Durham's mining past is so prevalent that the Durham Miners' Gala continues to be held annually in the city, despite the fact that the industry no longer exists locally. Much of the local coalfield was owned by the 3rd Marquis of Londonderry, Charles Vane Tempest, whose statue can be seen in the Market Place. He created the port at Seaham on what has become the Durham Heritage Coast (see page 66), an amazing stretch of regenerated coastline a few miles to the east of the city with a variety of magnificent landscapes and a splendid coastal walk.

▲ *View over the city from Wharton Park*

When to go

SEASONS & CLIMATE

The climate of the northeast of England is similar to the rest of eastern England, if a little cooler than areas to the south, especially during the summer. Average winter temperatures are around 3–5°C (37–41°F), while during the summer the average is around 16°C (61°F) although it often reaches about 20°C (68°F) or higher. However, the temperature in the Upper Dales is likely to be much lower. Rainfall is fairly evenly spread throughout the year but the driest months are from February to July. The best of the sunshine is generally from May to August. Durham is a year-round city with many places open during the winter.

ANNUAL EVENTS

Several popular events are held every year in Durham. Celebrating the written word at venues throughout the city, writers and poets such as Bill Bryson and Ian McMillan flood the city throughout late October for the **Durham Book Festival** (ⓦ www.durhambookfestival.com), while in May, local writers reinvent ancient biblical stories for **Durham Mystery Plays** (ⓦ www.durhammysteries.co.uk), incorporating contemporary dance, poetry and song, alongside traditional approaches.

The **Durham Festival and Regatta** (ⓦ www.durham-regatta.org.uk), dubbed the 'Henley of the North', is the second oldest rowing event in England and takes place in mid-June. With more than 600 crews taking part, this is the premier rowing event in the North of England. The regatta is followed in July with **Brass: Durham International Music Festival**

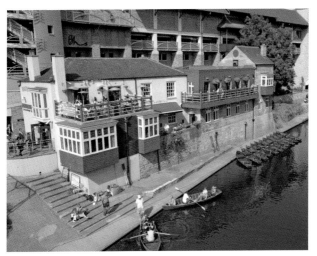

ⓦ www.brassfestival.co.uk, which sees brass bands from all over the city with jazz, funk, classical and ska, as well as traditional marches. The festival coincides with the Durham Miners' Gala, a long-standing annual event that began in 1871, when the bands join the marchers. Mining lodges from around the region take part in the gala, parading their silk banners through the city. Expect stirring speeches by prominent left-wing figures; in recent years politicians Tony Benn and Ken Livingstone have both spoken.

From early December, the **Durham City Christmas Festival**, a Victorian tradition, is held in the city centre with a children's lantern procession to Palace Green and carols in the cathedral.

▲ Hire a pleasure craft from Brown's Boathouse

History

Durham was founded in AD 995 by monks looking for a safe haven in which to bury the body of St Cuthbert, which they had brought from Lindisfarne. Legend has it that St Cuthbert appeared to them in a dream and told them to head for Dunholm – *dun* from the Anglo-Saxon meaning 'hill', and *holm* from the Norse meaning 'island'. The monks, not knowing where Dunholm was, wandered until they came across a milkmaid who had lost a 'dun' cow, last seen at Dunholm. This led them to the site of what would become the cathedral. The old name of Dunholm would be changed to Duresme after the Norman invasion, before being finally anglicised to Durham.

Before the Normans, however, came a Scottish invasion in AD 1006. It was repulsed and the heads of the invaders were gruesomely displayed around the city, earning the local people a fearsome reputation. In 1069, this reputation was reinforced when a small Norman army was slaughtered in the city. This led King William to commence the notorious 'Harrying of the North' and he quickly established his hold over the area, appointing a warrior bishop who ruled with a rod of iron from the castle. Referred to as prince bishops, these warriors were effectively kings in their own right and governed the North harshly.

Throughout the Middle Ages, Durham was a place of pilgrimage, despite being caught up in the Scottish Wars. In fact, the battle of Neville's Cross (1346), where a large Scottish army was heavily defeated by a small English force, was fought just to the west of the city. After the Reformation, the area was drawn into unrest yet again, notably the Pilgrimage of Grace (1536) and the Rising of the North (1569) led by northern Roman Catholic families. However, it gradually recovered and would go on to become a booming market town.

From the 17th century until relatively recently, Durham was at the centre of the local coal industry and was essentially defined by it. The Durham Miners' Gala is still an important annual event, despite the demise of the industry. Today, Durham is known largely as a university city and the institution founded in 1832 goes from strength to strength.

◆ *The great bronze 'sanctuary knocker' on the cathedral door*

Culture

As a renowned seat of learning and religion, Durham has long been a significant cultural centre. The castle and cathedral complex was granted UNESCO World Heritage status in 1986 due not only to its architectural significance but also to its cultural and religious importance over the past millennium. The Treasures of St Cuthbert Museum contains not only the relics of St Cuthbert but also the cathedral's original 11th-century doorknocker, among other artefacts.

Its famous university, the third oldest in England, is currently ranked by the *Complete University Guide* as the fourth best university in the UK. The university's Chancellor is Durham aficionado Bill Bryson, and famous alumni include TV journalist George Alagiah, athlete Jonathan Edwards, and Tim Smit, creator of the Eden Project.

Much more recent additions to the city are the **Gala Theatre** (see page 56), which hosts a full range of theatrical productions, and the **Oriental Museum** (see page 58), which is the only museum in the country dedicated to Oriental Art. The Durham Book Fair, held every October, serves to confirm Durham as one of the country's leading cultural centres.

● *The castle keep, now part of University College*

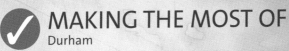

MAKING THE MOST OF
Durham

Shopping

As a market town, Durham city has always been an important centre for shopping, especially for people from the surrounding villages. In common with many cities, most traditional shops have long-since gone, replaced by high street chains that have themselves recently been augmented by two shopping centres in the heart of the city. The biggest attraction of shopping in Durham is the relaxed and rather cosy ambience created by the compact nature of the city centre. Most people's needs are catered for here but for those who need a full-on retail experience then the Metro Centre and Newcastle's Eldon Square are about 30 minutes away!

WHERE TO SHOP
Prince Bishops open-air shopping centre is the newest of the centres and is situated just off the Market Place, with more than 40 retail outlets selling everything from fashions to home ware. **The Gates**, also in the heart of the city, beside Framwellgate Bridge, has over 40 shops lining its indoor malls selling an extensive range of goods. **Saddler Street** and **Silver Street** are the main shopping streets, both having a good selection of shops and remaining very popular, especially the latter, which is fully pedestrianised.

WHAT TO BUY
There are no particular regional specialities, but the **Durham Indoor Market**, which has an entrance on the Market Place, houses over 50 independent traders offering a range of services and local food.

MARKETS

The Durham Indoor Market is a permanent feature of the city's shopping experience, but there are other markets that occur on a regular basis. Every Saturday, 30 stalls pop up in the Market Place, selling fresh produce and other goods, while a farmers' market takes place every third Thursday. Twice a year, in spring and autumn, the Market Place gets taken over by a four-day continental market.

🔺 *The Durham Indoor Market*

Eating & drinking

In recent years, eating out has become a much more important part of the local culture and, as a result, many new restaurants have opened up both in the city and the surrounding areas. Walkergate, adjacent to Millennium Place, offers a multicultural mix of eateries from Mexican to Portuguese and Italian to Asian. This complex has proved to be very popular with the locals and is ideally placed for theatre- and cinema-goers. The city's other restaurants are spread throughout the historic streets and further out, but generally within walking distance of the centre.

When looking for a place to eat, look for the 'TasteDurham' food quality mark displayed in windows. This is a national standard awarded by Visit England to restaurants, based on their menus and the quality of their food and the premises. Go to ⓦ www.tastedurham.co.uk for more on the award criteria and a complete list of award-holding restaurants. Restaurants are generally open at lunchtime from 12.00 to about 14.30, and in the evening from 19.00 to 22.30 or 23.00. Tipping is up to you – if you receive very good service then it will be appreciated; however, it is not necessary.

Pubs are normally open until 23.00. For those who prefer traditional ales, there are some microbreweries in the area, which produce beers with names that speak of their local heritage, like St Cuthbert, White Bishop, Bede's Gold, Sanctuary and Canny Lad (meaning 'nice young man' in the local dialect). If you fancy a picnic, the best place to eat alfresco is somewhere on the riverbank or perhaps up in Wharton Park, where you can enjoy a splendid view of the castle and cathedral.

⬤ *Elvet Bridge has a number of restaurants*

Entertainment

Unlike neighbouring Newcastle upon Tyne, Durham has never been known as a party city, or for that matter for the varied nature of its evening entertainment; although, due partly to having a large student population, the city has always been well served with pubs.

However, the addition of the Gala Theatre and Cinema and the Walkergate complex over the last few years has changed considerably the way the city is viewed as a place to go to be entertained. While, in terms of the variety and quantity of entertainment venues, it will never be a serious rival to the larger cities in the North, it has carved out a niche for itself as somewhere you can enjoy good food, see a play starring well-known actors or a concert touring the country and then relax with a late-night drink afterwards, all without walking more than a few metres in a very safe environment!

There are plenty of pubs scattered throughout the rest of the city, especially on Claypath, Saddler Street, Old Elvet and North Road, and some of these have regular comedy nights and bands playing on certain evenings. There is also the City Theatre based in Fowlers Yard in Back Silver Street, where an amateur group of players put on up to five productions per year to great acclaim (ⓦ www.durham-city-theatre.co.uk), and during the summer there are occasional Shakespearian productions by touring professional players staged at Durham Castle. If, however, you are unable to find anything to your taste in Durham on a particular evening, then it is but a short train ride or car journey along the A1(M) to Newcastle, where the choice is almost endless!

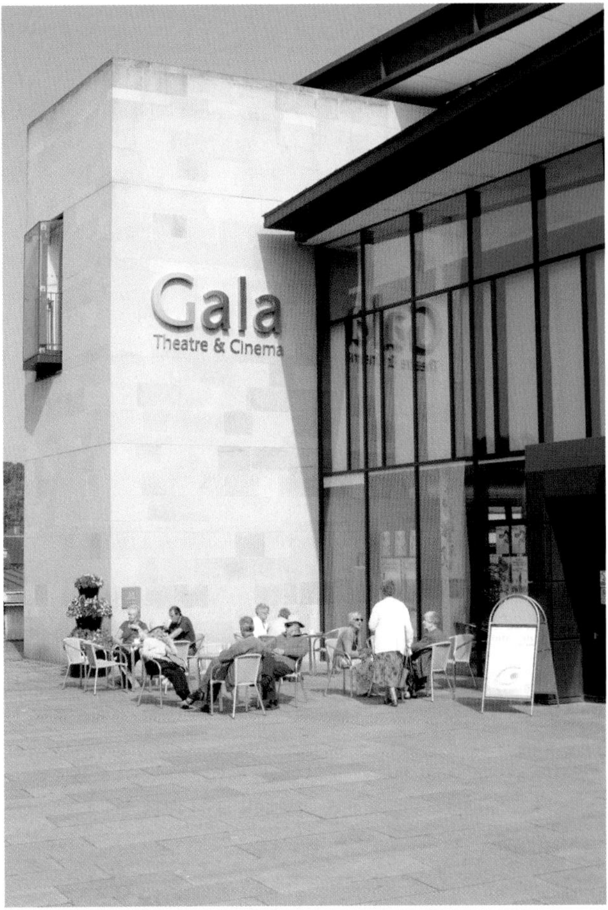

The centrepiece of Durham's arts programme

Sport & relaxation

Cricket

The sound of leather on willow as bat hits ball has always been very popular in the Durham area and most Durham villages have their own side. The major team in the area is Durham County Cricket Club based at Chester-le-Street, about 14 km (8¾ miles) from Durham city. The club has been hugely successful in recent years, becoming LV County Champions in 2008 and 2009. Several England internationals, such as Stephen Harmison, Paul Collingwood and Graham Onions, play regularly for the first team. ⓐ Emirates Durham International Ground, Chester-le-Street ⓣ 0191 387 1717 ⓦ www.durhamccc.co.uk ⓝ Bus: 21; train: Chester-le-Street station

Football

Durham city has not had a team in the Football League since 1928 and most football fans in the area support either Newcastle United or Sunderland. Durham City AFC, based just outside the centre at Belmont, plays in the Northern Premier League, winning this league in the 2008–9 season. ⓐ Esh Group Stadium, Belmont Industrial Estate ⓦ http://durhamcityafc.com ⓝ Bus: 65, 154, 220

Swimming

Located in the Walkergate Complex at Freeman's Quay, this new leisure-centre facility includes an eight-lane swimming pool, which is ideal for a relaxing swim. ⓷ Walkergate ⓣ 0191 301 8306 ⓦ www.activedurham.co.uk ⓛ 06.30–22.30 Mon–Fri, 08.30–19.30 Sat & Sun ⓘ Admission charge

Walking

There are several footpaths along the riverbank and to the south of the peninsula (see page 52). Out of town the possibilities are endless, with miles of former railway tracks having been converted into countryside paths. The new Durham Heritage Coastal Footpath (see page 69), linking Seaham to Crimdon Dene, offers 18 km (11 miles) of stunning trails along the beautiful Heritage Coast. Ⓦ www.activedurham.co.uk

◆ *Emirates Durham International Cricket Ground*

Accommodation

There is a good range of accommodation from boutique hotels to country houses, in both the city and the surrounding area, to suit all budgets and needs. From sumptuous 5-star serviced apartments and 4-star hotels to 1-star guesthouses, many are Visit Britain or AA assessed (sometimes both), helping to ensure that high standards are maintained. In recent years, in addition to the old established hotels that have been in business for many years, some new chain hotels have opened branches in and around Durham. Like most destinations, Durham can be very busy, particularly when there are events on in the area, so it is advisable to book in advance if at all possible. Having said this, provided you are flexible in your requirements, then you will probably find a room somewhere – even if it is outside the city centre.

Cathedral View Town House £ This bed and breakfast is located in a Grade II-listed Georgian town house with views of the cathedral, and is only a few minutes' walk from the Market Place. Excellent breakfasts with freshly home-made bread. ⓐ 212 Gilesgate ⓣ 0191 386 9566 ⓦ www.cathedralview.com ⓔ cathedralview@hotmail.com

Cuthbert's Rest £ A small, family-run B&B about 10 minutes' walk from the centre of Durham. All rooms have a shared bathroom and there is a guest lounge. Special dietary requirements catered for on request. ⓐ 42 Oswald Court ⓣ 0191 384 0405

Durham YHA £ Very basic twin en-suite accommodation is based in one of the university colleges very close to the cathedral. ⓐ St Chads College, 18 North Bailey ⓣ 0191 334 3358 ⓦ www.dur.ac.uk/StChads ⓛ Available July–Sept and other university holiday periods only

Moorcroft Bed & Breakfast £ Situated in an Edwardian house, about five minutes by car from the city centre, Moorcroft offers two well-equipped rooms, one en-suite and one with private bathroom. Choice of breakfast with vegetarian option is available. ⓐ Moor End, Belmont ⓣ 0191 386 7677

Premier Inn Durham North £ Located five minutes (by car) north of the city in the quaintly named village of Pity Me, this budget hotel offers clean, comfortable rooms and a friendly, efficient service. ⓐ Arnison Retail Centre, Pity Me ⓣ 0871 527 8342 ⓦ www.premierinn.com

66 Claypath ££ This listed Georgian House with a secluded garden is situated on Claypath, one of the historic routes into Durham. All rooms have double beds and are well equipped. Choice of breakfast, with special dietary needs catered for on request. ⓐ 66 Claypath ⓣ 0191 384 3193 ⓦ www.66claypath. co.uk ⓔ richard@66claypath.co.uk

Best Western Hardwick Hotel ££ One of the most beautifully situated country house hotels in County Durham, standing in 120 acres of Parkland. Once the home of Lord Boyne, it dates back to the 13th century and – following a £4-million investment

– the stylishly furnished rooms have many high-tech extras.
ⓐ Sedgefield, Durham ⓣ 0174 062 0253 ⓦ www.best
western.co.uk ⓔ info@hardwickhallhotel.co.uk

Castle View Guest House ££ A 250-year-old house close to the
centre with superb views of the cathedral and castle, with five
comfortable, well-equipped en-suite rooms. ⓐ 4 Crossgate
ⓣ 0191 386 8852 ⓦ www.castle-view.co.uk ⓔ info@guest
housedurham.co.uk

Durham Cottages ££ Two cottages in Gilesgate, Fern Cottage
and Rose Cottage, just ten minutes' walk from the city centre.
Both Grade II-listed buildings have accommodation for two
people. A third cottage, Dove Cottage, is available in Sherburn
Village, about 5 km (3 miles) out. ⓐ Gilesgate ⓣ 0191 372 1810
ⓦ www.durhamcottages.com ⓔ enquiries@durham
cottages.com

Grafton House ££ This boutique hotel, located in arguably the
smartest street in Durham, South Street, above the river Wear,
has stunning views of the cathedral and the castle. There are
nine individually designed rooms, with chic and contemporary
bespoke furniture. ⓐ 40 South Street ⓣ 0191 375 6790
ⓦ www.grafton-house.co.uk ⓔ stay@grafton-house.co.uk

The Ramside Hall Classic Hotel and Golf Club ££ Only 3.2 km
(2 miles) from the centre of Durham, this family-owned hotel
offers comfortable and spacious rooms, set in beautiful
parkland with 27 holes of championship golf. ⓐ Carrville,

Durham ☎ 0191 386 5282 ⊕ www.ramsidehallhotel.co.uk
⊜ mail@ramsidehallhotel.co.uk

The Victorian Town House ££ This renovated Victorian property
overlooking Wharton Park is only 5 minutes from the city centre.
All the rooms are furnished to a high standard and well
equipped. Choice of breakfast. ⓐ Victoria Terrace ☎ 0191 370
9963 ⊕ www.durhambedandbreakfast.com ⊜ stay@durham
bedandbreakfast.com

Durham City Apartment £££ A spacious, contemporary
fifth-floor two-bedroomed apartment with lift service
located beside the river in the Walkergate Complex.
ⓐ 32 Freemans Quay, Walkergate ☎ 0191 371 9060
⊕ www.durhamcityapartment.co.uk ⊜ enquiries@durham
cityapartment.co.uk

Durham Marriott Hotel Royal County £££ Four-star luxury in the
heart of Durham city, on the banks of the river Wear and with fine
views of the castle and cathedral. Formerly the venerable Royal
County Hotel where Oliver Cromwell is reputed to have stayed.
ⓐ Old Elvet ☎ 0191 386 6821 ⊕ www.marriott.co.uk

The Radisson Blu Hotel £££ On the riverside in the heart of the
city, this AA 4-star-rated establishment with 207 contemporary
rooms offers everything you would expect, including a health
club, treatment rooms and a pool. ⓐ Framwellgate Waterside
☎ 0191 372 7200 ⊕ www.radissonblu.co.uk/hotel-durham
⊜ info.durham@radissonsas.com

THE BEST OF DURHAM

The centre of Durham is very compact and the main city sights can be seen comfortably in a day.

TOP 10 ATTRACTIONS

- **Durham Cathedral** This outstanding Romanesque structure, set high upon the peninsula, dominates the city (see pages 45–7).

- **Durham Castle** Sharing the city skyline with the cathedral is the magnificent medieval castle, which was built for the prince bishops (see pages 44–5).

- **Durham Indoor Market** A charming Victorian market with over 50 local independent traders (see pages 47–8).

- **Silver Street and Saddler Street.** Both these ancient streets lead from the Market Place, the former to Framwellgate Bridge and the latter to the cathedral (see pages 53–5).

- **Botanic Garden** A peaceful garden set among woodland on the southern edge of the city and containing plants from around the world (see pages 42–3).

- **Boat trip on the Wear** Hire a rowing boat or take a leisurely lunch and cruise on board the *Prince Bishop* river cruiser (see page 39).

- **The Gala Theatre** The purpose-built Gala Theatre & Cinema on Millennium Place has a spacious café bar and hosts the very best entertainment (see page 56).

- **Framwellgate Bridge and Elvet Bridge** Two Grade-I-listed medieval structures on opposite sides of the peninsula (see pages 50–53).

- **The Bowes Museum (Teesdale)** A magnificently surprising 19th-century French-style château with artworks by no less than El Greco and Canaletto (see pages 84–5).

- **High Force (Teesdale)** This dramatic unbroken waterfall has a drop of over 21 m (70 ft) (see page 81).

The River Wear at Durham

Suggested itineraries

HALF-DAY: DURHAM IN A HURRY

Even for a small city like Durham, half a day is not enough time
to see the place properly, but it will certainly allow you to see
enough to want to return. From the **Market Place**, walk up
towards **Durham Cathedral** and stroll around **Palace Green** in
order to appreciate the surrounding architecture. Take a close
look at the replica **sanctuary knocker** as you enter the cathedral
and admire the view along the Nave. If time allows, walk down
from Palace Green to the **riverside path** and enjoy the serenity
created by the water and the trees around the peninsula.

1 DAY: TIME TO SEE A LITTLE MORE

Follow the first part of the half-day recommendation and then
visit the **Galilee Chapel**, before heading along the North Aisle
past the North Transept to **St Cuthbert's shrine**. Return along
the South Aisle to the cloisters. Stop a moment to admire the
massive central tower and then visit the **Monks' Dormitory** and
the Treasures of St Cuthbert. Later, take a guided tour of the
castle, and then head down to the riverside path and enjoy the
classic view from **Prebends Bridge**.

2–3 DAYS: SHORT CITY BREAK

If day one is spent as suggested above, then the second and
third days can be spent looking around the museums and
exploring the historic parts of the city. A walk up **Silver Street**,
through the **Market Place** to **Saddler Street**, and on to North
and South Bailey could well be coupled with visits to the

Heritage Centre and the **Old Fulling Mill**. On the final day, see the **Durham Light Infantry (DLI) Museum**, making a detour into **Wharton Park** to enjoy the panoramic view of the city before later taking in the **Oriental Museum**.

LONGER: ENJOYING DURHAM TO THE FULL

If you are fortunate enough to have longer then you will be able to enjoy long lunches in one of many pleasant restaurants or even on the river (see page 39) and perhaps visit the Victorian Durham **Indoor Market** before looking around the **Town Hall** next door. There will be time, too, to visit the **Heritage Coast** and the **Dales**, probably allocating one day for each one.

🔺 *Framwellgate Bridge is Durham's oldest*

Something for nothing

The peninsula on which Durham city is built provides what have to be some of the best city-centre walks in the UK. A well-chosen route along the banks of the River Wear can be completely car free, and, even in the height of summer, not too crowded. Best of all, it is absolutely free! There are several points where the **riverside path** can be accessed, but one of the best is by descending the steps from either side of the medieval Framwellgate Bridge and heading south along the riverbank to Prebends Bridge. Take the right bank and climb up on to the bridge where you can admire both the view of the river, the cathedral and the plaque with Sir Walter Scott's famous 'Grey towers of Durham' inscription from his poem 'Harold the Dauntless' on the bridge wall.

From here you can continue along the river, underneath the modern, reinforced-concrete Kingsgate Bridge and the medieval Elvet Bridge, both Grade I listed, or return to Framwellgate Bridge by a path higher up the riverbank.

There are also several attractions that can be entered free. There is no charge to look around **Durham Cathedral**, although you have to pay to climb the Tower and to see some exhibitions. Also on Palace Green, and free to enter, is the **University Library** and other buildings nearby housing the Archives and Special Collections. Arguably the best view of the city centre can be obtained by taking a short walk from the centre into **Wharton Park**. Among the children's play area and mini-golf there is a viewing platform from which there is a panoramic view featuring castle and cathedral.

When it rains

The magnificent **cathedral** is the ideal place to visit when it rains. Even if the bad weather persists all day, there is sufficient to keep the visitor's interest, especially if you decide to have lunch in the charming Undercroft Restaurant located in the cloisters. The **castle** also provides a nice sheltered visit hosted by one of the university students. While the Keep is out of bounds, due to being a student residence, there is sufficient of interest to keep the visitor engaged and, perhaps more importantly, dry for at least an hour. Nearby, **The Gates** and the **Durham Indoor Market**, while relatively small, provide adequate shelter from the rain, not to mention some good shopping opportunities. In addition, they are quite close to each other so it is possible to get from one to the other without getting too wet! The **Durham Heritage Centre and Museum**, located in a deconsecrated historic church, stands beside the cathedral on North Bailey and is the best place to find out about the history of the city since its very founding.

Just out of the centre of the city at Aykley Heads, there is the fascinating **Durham Light Infantry Museum**, celebrating the history of the famous regiment that served with great distinction during numerous campaigns, including the Crimean War and both world wars. Together with its contemporary art gallery, the museum will fascinate the visitor for at least a couple of hours. If poor weather persists, then there are plenty of interesting sights and attractions not far out of the city to the west, including the unique **Bowes Museum** in Teesdale, with its fascinating, recently renovated fish-eating Silver Swan!

On arrival

ARRIVING
By air
Newcastle International Airport is 40 km (25 miles) north of Durham centre and the journey time by car is 30 to 40 minutes depending upon traffic conditions. The Tyne and Wear Metro system operates regular services from the airport and takes you straight into Newcastle city centre, from where you can take the train or bus to Durham. Metro Trains leave every 12 minutes and the journey time to Newcastle is 25 minutes. Buses (X77, X78, X79) take 18 minutes to Eldon Square and run every 30 minutes Mon–Sat. However, they do not call in at the airport, but pass on the main road outside (B6918). By far the best method to get to Newcastle city centre is by Metro Train or to take one of the readily available taxis, which operate from outside the Arrivals Hall. There are car rental offices in the Arrivals Hall as well as a bureau de change and an information desk.

Durham Tees Valley Airport is 39 km (24 miles) south of Durham and the journey time by car is about 35 minutes. There is no bus service to Durham directly; however, there is one that runs hourly and connects the airport with Darlington (🔵 Bus: 12), from which there is a choice of taxis or a very regular train service that runs to Durham. There are car rental offices in the Arrivals Hall, as well as two Travelex shops on site.

By rail
Durham Station is just a few minutes' walk from the centre of the city and is well served by express trains from London

⬤ *Silver Street, heading to Framwellgate Bridge*

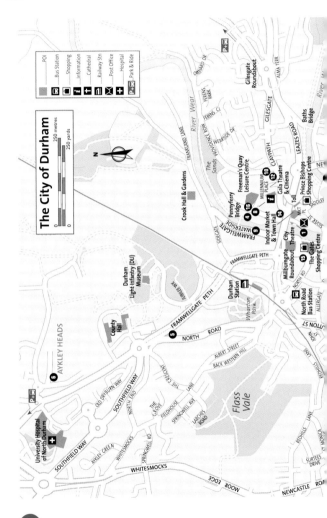

The City of Durham

	POI
🚌	Bus Station
🛍	Shopping
ℹ	Information
⌂	Cathedral
🚉	Railway Stn
✉	Post Office
✕	Hospital
P&R	Park & Ride

0   250 metres
0   250 yards

N

River Wear

Crook Hall & Gardens

FRANKLAND LANE

The Sands

FERENS PARK

FERENS CL

PROVIDENCE ROW

WEARSIDE DR

ORCHARD DR

Gilesgate Roundabout

ALMA TER

GILESGATE

CLAYPATH

LEAZES ROAD

Baths Bridge

River W

Freeman's Quay Leisure Centre

Pennyferry Bridge

MILLENNIUM PLACE

Gala Theatre & Cinema

Prince Bishops Shopping Centre

Toll

SADDLER

SILVER S

Indoor Market & Town Hall

FRAMWELLGATE WATERSIDE

SIDEGATE

City Theatre

MKT PL

The Gates Shopping Centre

Millburngate Roundabout

FRAMWELLGATE PETH

NORTH RD

North Road Bus Station

ALLERGATE

SUTTON ST

JOHN ST

STINGER LANE

Durham Light Infantry (DLI) Museum

FRAMWELLGATE PETH

HUBBLE WK

Durham Station

Wharton Park

County Hall

AYKLEY HEADS

NORTH ROAD

ALBERT STREET

BACK WESTERN HILL

THE CRESCENT

OLD SPENNITHORN WAY

NORTH END

SOUTHFIELD WAY

University Hospital of North Durham

SOUTHFIELD WAY

AYKLEY GREEN

WHITESMOCKS

SPRINGWELL RD

THE GROVE

FIELDHOUSE LANE

SPRINGWELL AVE

LARCHES ROAD

Flass Vale

KEPIER LANE

ST MONICA

SURTEES DRIVE

MOOR EDGE

WHITESMOCKS

NEWCASTLE ROA

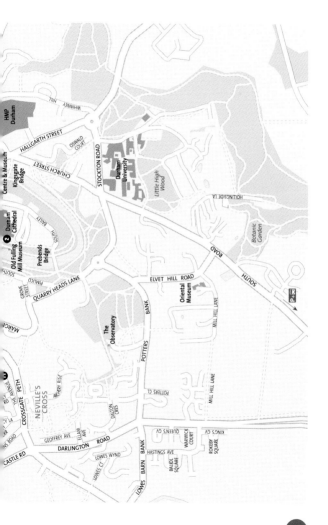

(journey time about 3 hours), Manchester and Edinburgh. Some hotels are within walking distance of the station but taxis operate from the car park outside.

By coach
National Express coaches operate to and from North Road Bus Station. There are several services daily from London (journey time approximately 6 to 7 hours 30 minutes) and from other cities.

By car
Durham is approached from the north and the south by the A1(M) or by the A167 and there are signs to the city centre from both directions. From the west, use the A66, which joins the A1(M) heading northbound at Scotch Corner. Durham is a small, well-signposted city so driving is not difficult and there are usually plenty of car parking spaces available. There are six surface car parks and three multi-storey car parks, as well as nearly 1,700 on-street spaces. Details of off-street parking facilities can be found by going to ⓦ www.durham.gov.uk Parking fees are quite reasonable, but note: it is best to avoid parking in restricted areas as the regulations are strictly enforced.

FINDING YOUR FEET
Like their Geordie neighbours in Newcastle, Durham people are generally very friendly and welcoming. They are proud of their city and Wearside's considerable industrial and cultural heritage, which is significantly different to that of nearby Tyneside,

◆ Old Shire Hall dominates elegant Old Elvet

especially with respect to the local accent and sporting loyalties. In general, people are very willing to help visitors whenever they can, but bear in mind that at times there are so many students and visitors in the centre that you may have to persevere to find a local. Being very compact, the centre is easy to become familiar with, meaning that the visitor will feel at home almost immediately. With respect to dress, there are no hard and fast rules. Eating places are relaxed about this and even in the more sophisticated establishments, informal clothing is acceptable and tends to be the norm.

Durham is a very safe city with levels of street crime having fallen significantly in recent years. Although there are occasionally minor incidents, these are very rare and there are fewer such crimes than in comparable places. Also, although the centre does attract its fair share of young people to the many pubs and clubs in the evenings, especially at weekends, it is still a perfectly safe environment in which to enjoy the varied 'after dark' attractions. Having said this, it is always a good idea to take all the normal precautions you would usually when visiting any city or town.

Streets in the centre, including the Market Place, are closed to most vehicular traffic and there is very little traffic on the peninsula itself. However, care does need to be taken as there may be delivery vehicles about and traffic is allowed on to Palace Green on payment of the congestion charge. Streets beyond the peninsula are open to traffic in the normal way.

ORIENTATION

It is not difficult to orientate yourself in the city, partly because of its size and partly because the landmarks are obvious. You can, if you wish, use the services of the tour guides who know the city well (Ⓦ www.thisisdurham.com) or head straight for the excellent tourist information centre, located beside the Gala Theatre in Millennium Place in order to obtain a map and information on the sights you wish to see. There are no open-top bus tours or similar rides in Durham, but there is the possibility of a trip along a section of the Wear on the *Prince Bishop* river cruiser (Ⓦ www.princebishoprc.co.uk).

   A good place to start is the Market Place, with its striking equestrian statue of the Marquis of Londonderry just a short walk down Claypath from Millennium Place. From here you can easily reach all the sights and attractions on foot. The cathedral and castle are the main landmarks, of course, since they can be seen from most places, but the river also can help you to orientate yourself once you get used to the fact that it forms a tight loop around the city. From Framwellgate Bridge to Elvet Bridge via the Market Place, where the loop is at its narrowest, it is only about 250 m (273 yards) from riverbank to riverbank. Another good place to get a sense of the city and the way it is laid out is to cross the river and, from the Millburngate traffic island, head up Framwellgate Peth. From Wharton Park, above the railway station, you will be able to enjoy an extensive panorama, including the castle and cathedral with the old town below.

GETTING AROUND

It is easy to cover Durham city on foot, due to the relatively small size of the centre, and it takes no more than 20 minutes or so to get from one side of the city to the other and about 10 minutes to walk the length of the peninsula. If you are staying outside the city there are three Park-and-Ride car parks, but note that this facility operates only from 07.00 to 19.00 Monday to Saturday.

'Out of town' trips to the Durham Heritage Coast and The Durham Dales are easy to make by car; they are also accessible by bus, but the journey times – especially to the Dales – are quite long. Using the train is not an option. The Metro Centre can be reached by car in about 20 minutes, by train via Newcastle or by bus from North Road Bus Station in Durham. The outlet centre at Dalton Park can be reached by bus from Durham in 45 minutes and by car in about 20 minutes.

Car hire

If you plan to spend all your time in Durham itself then you don't need to hire a car. If, however, you wish to visit some outlying areas, including perhaps the Durham Heritage Coast or The Durham Dales, then you would be well advised to do so. All the usual car-rental companies can be found in the area. It may even be a good idea to book a car before you arrive, especially at busy times, but if you have been unable to do this, your hotel should be able to help you.

▶ *River Wear, Framwellgate Bridge, the castle and cathedral*

THE CITY OF
Durham

The City of Durham

Durham is a superb small city with most of its magnificent places of interest located on the peninsula formed by a loop in the River Wear as it passes through the city on its journey from the Pennines in the west to nearby Sunderland and the North Sea in the east.

Unlike its neighbour Newcastle, Durham was not planned, but rather has grown organically around the hill on which the castle and cathedral are built, and because of this has retained its unique charm and almost medieval ambience.

Almost all of the main places of interest are actually on the peninsula itself, and those that are not, such as Crook Hall and Wharton Park, are mostly within ten minutes' walk from the Market Place.

SIGHTS & ATTRACTIONS

Botanic Garden

Belonging to the university, this quiet, 9-hectare (22-acre) garden, set in beautiful woodlands just a short distance from the city centre, is one of Durham's most popular attractions. On view are plant collections from around the world, including China, Japan, North America, Chile, South Africa and New Zealand, themed gardens and a splendid Monkey Puzzle tree. There are even tropical rainforest plants and insects, including scorpions and tarantulas. An unusual feature is that from late summer to early spring the arboretum is grazed by rare-breed sheep, which greatly benefits the wild flowers and insects that flourish there. ⓐ Hollingside Lane ⓣ 0191 334 5521

🌐 www.dur.ac.uk/botanic.garden 🕐 10.00–17.00 daily
(Mar–Oct); 10.00–16.00 daily (Nov–Feb) ❶ Admission charge

Crook Hall & Gardens

This Grade-I-listed medieval hall and associated buildings, which
once served as a family home, are surrounded by stunning
gardens and are only a short walk from the Market Place.
Described by *Country Life* as having 'history, romance and beauty',
the gardens include a maze, a Moat Pool, together with a Secret
Walled Garden and a Shakespeare Garden. Home-made cream
teas are served and special events held throughout the year.

🔺 *The peaceful Botanic Garden*

🅐 Frankland Lane, Sidegate ☎ 0191 384 8028 🅦 www. crookhall gardens.co.uk 🕐 11.00–17.00 Sun–Thur (Apr–Sept); check website for other times and special events ⓘ Admission charge

Durham Castle

Returning from Scotland in 1072, William the Conqueror ordered a motte-and-bailey castle to be built here and the work was carried out by the Saxon Earl of Northumberland, Waltheof. The

🔺 *Crook Hall is surrounded by tranquil themed gardens*

castle was occupied by the 'prince bishops' who ruled the North on the king's behalf and who gradually added to and restored the building. The Great Hall, now used as a dining hall by the university, was begun in 1284 by Bishop Bek and completed by Bishop Hatfield in the mid-14th century, while the adjacent kitchens were completed by Bishop Fox in 1499. The western and northern wings of the castle, which include the Bishop's Suite and Dining Room, were joined by Bishop Cosin's Black Staircase of 1662, widely regarded as one of the best in the country at the time. However, the most impressive part of the castle, the Keep, was originally built in the 14th century by Bishop Hatfield, but fell into disrepair and was rebuilt in the mid-19th century to house the students of the new university. Even today, some fortunate students have rooms here. The whole building is now known as University College, sometimes affectionately as 'Castle', and should you choose to look around it is likely to be one of the resident students who guides you. To visit the interior, which also includes a charming Norman chapel, enter the courtyard through Bishop Pudsey's 12th-century Gatehouse. ⓐ Palace Green ① 0191 334 3800 ⓦ www.dur.ac.uk/university.college ⓛ Guided tours: 14.00, 15.00, 16.00 Mon–Fri (university term time); 10.00, 11.00, 12.00, 14.00, 15.00, 16.00, 17.00 (university vacations) ⓘ Admission charge

Durham Cathedral

The Romanesque cathedral is the jewel in the city's crown and is widely regarded as one the best examples of Norman architecture in Europe. Constructed between 1093 and 1133, it was designated, together with the castle, a UNESCO World

Heritage Site in 1986. It is not difficult to understand why people have been in awe of this structure since its earliest days.

The cathedral, with its massive square 15th-century central tower, is on the southern edge of Palace Green. It was constructed at the same time as the castle to emphasise the power of the Norman conquerors and to house the remains of St Cuthbert, who was responsible for evangelising Northumbria. It also houses the body of the Venerable Bede, the 'father of English History'.

⬤ *The Rose Window over the Chapel of the Nine Altars*

Entering the cathedral by the North Porch door, you will notice a large bronze sanctuary knocker, which is in fact a replica, as the real one is exhibited inside. In medieval times, if a felon seeking safe haven could reach the knocker, they would be given sanctuary inside. Stand at the west end of the Nave and try to imagine how awestruck a medieval person would be when confronted with the sheer size and beauty of the interior. At the west end is the Galilee Chapel, built in the late 12th century and from 1370 home of the tomb of the Venerable Bede. This light, airy structure was a consistory court before becoming a school. At the other end of the cathedral, beyond the Quire with its beautifully carved stalls dating from the 17th century, and adjacent to the 13th-century Chapel of the Nine Altars, is the shrine of St Cuthbert. The restored Cloister, reached from the South Aisle of the Nave, provide access to the Treasury – which contains St Cuthbert's relics, the Library and also, for those in need of refreshment, the Undercroft Restaurant (see page 60). ☎ 0191 386 4266 Ⓦ www.durhamcathedral.co.uk 🕐 09.30–18.00 Mon–Sat, 12.30–17.30 Sun (until 20.00 mid-July–Aug); Library: 10.00–13.00, 14.00–16.00 Mon–Fri

Durham Indoor Market

This charming Victorian market was established in 1851 on the site of the old palace, which had originally belonged to the Neville family before being confiscated following their participation in the 1569 Rising of the North. In the early 19th century, there were so many traders in the Market Place it became unsafe, and so the new market hall was created. During the late-19th century, however, the market declined, opening

only once per week and for special sales. It was eventually refurbished with space for over 50 independent traders, and in 1996 was reopened by Tony Blair. Now it is a thriving market once more and is open six days a week. ⓐ Market Place
ⓣ 0191 384 6153 ⓦ www.durhammarkets.co.uk ⓛ 09.00–17.00 Mon–Sat

Market Place

Lying right at the heart of the commercial part of the city, the Market Place is known particularly for its two famous statues. The oldest is the statue of **Neptune**, which was erected in 1729 beside the public water supply, symbolising the impractical idea of making Durham an inland port by joining the Wear to the River Tyne, or by making the Wear navigable downriver to Sunderland. Neither plan came to fruition, although the 3rd **Marquis of Londonderry**, whose equestrian statue also

🔺 *In the Cloister walkway*

stands in the Market Place, did build a port at nearby Seaham (see page 69) from which to export his coal.

A small market does take place here on Saturdays, with more than 30 stalls selling fresh produce, but the main market is the Durham Indoor Market (see page 47). The 19th-century **Church of St Nicholas** also stands on the north side of the Market Place. It was built to replace a rather more attractive medieval church that stood on this site, forming part of the city walls and the now-demolished Clayport Gate. The most interesting thing about the newer church is that one of its former vicars was George Carey, who went on to become Archbishop of Canterbury. The **Town Hall** stands on the east side of the Market Place; it resembles a medieval structure, but in fact was built in 1851. It has a hammerbeam roof and there is an adjacent guildhall, which dates from 1665. Among the exhibits are some artefacts belonging to Count Joseph Burowalski, an accomplished violinist and mimic, who entertained Marie Antoinette, among others, before retiring to Durham in 1790. In his day, this tiny man, said to be 1 m (3 ft 3 in) tall, achieved great fame and he is buried in the cathedral under the initials 'JB'.

🅐 Market Place 🅣 0191 301 8499

Millennium Place

Millennium Place was created from a derelict brownfield site in 2001 as a 1,000-year birthday present for the city, linking the peninsula and Market Place with surrounding areas. A community-based initiative, it features the Gala Theatre & Cinema and a series of piazzas leading down to the river with a centre for lifelong learning and a riverside park. The most striking recent addition is a sculpture on the main piazza by local artist Fenwick Lawson, *The Journey*, which commemorates in bronze the journey taken by the Lindisfarne monks, carrying the remains of St Cuthbert to their eventual resting place in Durham Cathedral.

The old bridges

There are eight bridges in total over the River Wear at Durham, but only two are open to vehicular traffic. Of the remainder, three are of historical significance and have Grade I-listed status. The oldest is **Framwellgate Bridge**, leading from North Road to Silver Street. It was constructed around 1120 by Bishop Ranulf Flambard and known for many years as the 'Old Bridge'. Originally it had a tower and gateway at the Silver Street end, but this has long since disappeared. It was the scene of a notorious murder in 1318, when the bishop's steward was killed by Ralph Neville, the so-called 'Peacock of the North'. The structure was badly damaged by floods in the 15th century, but was rebuilt and carried vehicular traffic until the early 1970s.

On the opposite side of the peninsula is **Elvet Bridge**, leading from Saddler Street to Old Elvet across the river. Constructed by Bishop Pudsey in 1160, and often known as Pudsey's bridge, this structure linked the old town with the rapidly developing suburb of Elvet to the west. Like Framwellgate Bridge on the other side of the peninsula, Elvet Bridge also had to be rebuilt periodically, especially following the disastrous floods of 1771. It is now pedestrianised. Elvet Bridge is best seen from the riverbank, where it can be observed that there are seven arches,

The Mayor's Chamber in the Town Hall

of which three are over land. Like many old bridges, Elvet used to have houses on it, and if you look carefully you will notice that the first arch at the Elvet end still has a house on it – a rare phenomenon in England.

Between these two medieval bridges is the somewhat newer **Prebends Bridge**, which crosses the river just before it loops round the tip of the peninsula. Constructed in 1777 and named after the prebendaries, or honorary canons of the cathedral, this bridge links the southern part of the town with the peninsula. From this pedestrianised crossing there is perhaps the best possible view of the cathedral. A plaque on the side of the bridge bears the words of Sir Walter Scott:

◯ *Take a cruise on the* Prince Bishop

Grey towers of Durham,
Yet well I love thy mixed and massive piles
Half church of God, half castle 'gainst the Scot
And long to roam these venerable aisles
With records stored of deeds long since forgot.

Old Elvet and Old Shire Hall

Opposite Elvet Bridge lies Old Elvet, an elegant broad curving street lined with 18th-century houses, leading eventually to the notorious prison built in 1810 and still in use today. At the entrance to Old Elvet is the Marriott Royal County Hotel, whose balcony is used by trade union leaders and prominent Labour Party politicians to acknowledge the procession on Miner's Gala Day. Further along, however, is Old Elvet's crowning glory, the magnificent Grade-II-listed Victorian red-brick Old Shire Hall, built in 1895 to house the County Council. Since 1963, it has been the headquarters of Durham University, although there are plans to convert it into a luxury hotel when the university moves to new premises in 2012.

Saddler Street and Silver Street

Leading into the Market Place, both these ancient streets have a fascinating history and, although today Silver Street especially is lined with ubiquitous chain stores, they still give a good impression of how the lower town must have looked in earlier times.

Saddler Street heads south from the Market Place to North Bailey and is the way to the cathedral and castle. It was originally known as Saddlergate, although the lower part was also known as Flesher Gate, where cattle were slaughtered and the butchers' premises used to be located. The most famous resident of Saddler Street was a certain 'Mrs Mustard', or more correctly Mrs Clements, who, during the early 18th century, used to produce the famously strong Durham mustard, which sold all over England, from her factory here. About halfway up Saddler Street, the Magdelen Steps lead down to Elvet Bridge along what used to be known as Souter Peth, the old street of the cobblers.

Silver Street leads uphill from Framwellgate Bridge into the Market Place. Some say the name is derived from a mint that may have been located here in medieval times. Saddler Street may have had Mrs Mustard but Silver Street can boast the splendidly named Mr John Duck, who arrived penniless in

▲ *Looking down Saddler Street towards the Market Place*

Durham in 1655, but eventually became mayor of Durham and received a knighthood. His house was demolished in 1963.

While Silver Street has been pedestrianised since the 1970s, Saddler Street still has some traffic, although access is restricted to both the Market Place and Saddler Street following the implementation of the first congestion charge in the UK, in 2002.

Wharton Park

Originally the grounds of Dryburn Hall, the home of the Wharton family, this park on a hilltop overlooks the city; from the specially created battery viewing area there is a magnificent view of the cathedral and castle. In addition, the park has many of the features you would expect – floral displays, tennis courts, putting green, children's electric cars (summer only), a multi-use games area for older children and a play area with swings and a slide. ⓐ Entrances on North Road, Framwellgate Peth and from the train station

CULTURE

Durham Heritage Centre & Museum

At this fascinating museum, the story of Durham from medieval times to the modern era is told using interactive displays in the historic deconsecrated church of St Mary-le-Bow near the cathedral. Objects illustrating everyday life from the 17th century to the modern era are on display. ⓐ St Mary-le-Bow, North Bailey ☏ 0191 384 5589 ⓦ www.durhamheritage centre. org.uk ⓗ Hours vary – see website ⓘ Admission charge

Durham Light Infantry Museum

The Durham Light Infantry Museum, situated on the open parkland that was the site of the last colliery in Durham city, is only a short walk from the city centre. It celebrates the history of the county's own regiment, formed in 1758 and amalgamated with other regiments to become simply the Light Infantry in 1968. The DLI served with great distinction in the Crimean and both world wars, as well as in many other campaigns, and earned the praise of no less a soldier than Field Marshall Montgomery who said, 'There may be some regiments as good, but I know of none better.' ⓐ Aykley Heads ❶ 0191 384 2214 ⓦ www.durham.gov.uk/dli ❶ 10.00–17.00 daily (Apr–Oct); 10.00–16.00 daily (Nov–Mar) ❶ Admission charge

Gala Theatre & Cinema

The Gala is a magnificent, purpose-built complex on Millennium Place above the river, with state-of-the-art theatre facilities, a two-screen cinema and café-bar. A great variety of live events are offered, including productions by leading theatre companies, performances by comedians, bands and musicians representing all genres. The two-screen cinema shows a variety of films, including classics as well as the latest blockbusters. ⓐ Millennium Place ❶ 0191 332 4041 ⓦ www.galadurham.co.uk ❶ Check website for times

Old Fulling Mill Museum

Durham used to be an important cloth-making centre and the Old Fulling Mill was a key part of that. Situated below the cathedral on the banks of the river, it forms one of the classic

⬥ The Old Fulling Mill, now a museum

photographic images of the city, especially when viewed from Prebends Bridge. It is now the home of the university's archaeological collections, which focus on the rich heritage of the northeast of England. ⓐ The Banks ⓣ 0191 334 1823 ⓦ www.durham.ac.uk/fulling.mill ⓛ 11.00–16.00 daily (Apr–Oct); 11.30–15.30 Fri–Mon (Nov–Mar) ⓘ Admission charge

Oriental Museum

Belonging to Durham University and opened in 1960, this is the only museum in the North to specialise in Oriental art and archaeology. There are collections from Japan, China, India, East Asia and the Near and Middle East, as well as a year-round programme of exhibitions. ⓐ Elvet Hill ⓣ 0191 334 5694 ⓦ www.dur.ac.uk/oriental.museum ⓛ 10.00–17.00 Mon–Fri, 12.00–17.00 Sat, Sun & Bank Holidays ⓘ Admission charge

University Library & Archive

Housed in a cluster of buildings around Palace Green, the University Library Archive and Special Collections contains over 70,000 books printed before 1850, as well as ancient manuscripts, maps and artefacts. The Wolfson Hall exhibition gallery has an exhibition showcasing some of the treasures of Durham University's outstanding collections. Telephone first to enquire about viewing particular collections. ⓐ Palace Green ⓣ 0191 334 2972 ⓦ www.durham.ac.uk/library ⓛ 09.00–17.00 Mon–Fri, check the website for exhibition opening hours

RETAIL THERAPY

Durham is not a major shopping district but there are some good independent shops, which, together with the unusual Durham Indoor Market (🕐 09.00–17.00 Mon–Sat) and two shopping centres, make it an interesting place to shop.

Bramwells This family-run business is the UK's largest stockist of Pandora bracelets and charms and specialises in diamond rings and jewellery, watches and Frogman Frogs. The original shop on Elvet Bridge deals in second-hand jewellery. ⓐ 28 Prince Bishops Shopping Centre ☎ 0191 383 5793

La Cookshop One of the largest selections of Bridgewater ceramics in the northeast, as well as high-quality cookware, this shop specialises in everything for the kitchen. ⓐ 9 Saddler Street ☎ 0191 383 1722 ⓦ www.lacookshop.co.uk

Durham Indoor Market This charming Victorian market, established in 1851, has over 50 independent traders offering bargains and a unique shopping experience. In addition to the retail stalls, there are services such as clothing alterations, key cutting, engraving, jewellery and watch repairs and an award-winning Café Cenno with free Wi-Fi facilities upstairs. ⓐ Market Place ☎ 0191 384 6153 ⓦ www.durhammarkets.co.uk

Lebeado Beads Moroccan beads, bangles and bracelets to suit all budgets. ⓐ 89 Elvet Bridge ☎ 0191 370 9873 ⓦ www.lebeado.co.uk

The Mugwump Something for everyone in this boutique, with a selection of designer labels, soft toys, glassware, prints and greeting cards. ❸ 37 Saddler Street ❶ 0191 386 1282

Perkins Menswear from leading labels is offered here in addition to dress wear for purchase or hire. ❸ 71 North Road ❶ 0191 384 8527

TAKING A BREAK

From morning coffee to gourmet eating, Durham has an excellent selection of restaurants, cafés and other eateries, most of which boast the 'TasteDurham' quality mark, which means you can be sure of high standards.

Leonard's Coffee House £ ❶ This is the perfect place to chill after a hard morning's sightseeing, over a steaming cup of Fairtrade coffee and freshly prepared food. It's located in Fowlers Yard beside the river. ❸ 1 Back Silver Street, Fowlers Yard ❶ 0191 384 0647 Ⓦ www.leonardscoffeehouse.co.uk ❶ 08.00–17.00 Mon–Sat, 09.00–17.00 Sun

The Undercroft Restaurant £ ❷ Located in the cloisters of Durham Cathedral, the Undercroft offers an excellent selection of home-produced and, where possible, locally sourced food from sandwiches to traditional meals. ❸ The Cloisters, Durham Cathedral ❶ 0191 386 3721 Ⓦ www.durhamcathedral.co.uk ❶ 10.00–16.30 daily

Vennels Café £ ❸ Next to Waterstones up a vennel (alleyway), leading to a 16th-century courtyard, this café serves bread, cakes and quiches baked on site and is a favourite with locals. One of Durham's best-kept secrets. ⓐ Saddlers Yard, 71 Saddler Street

AFTER DARK

RESTAURANTS

Being a university city, Durham has a great deal going on during the evening, and the **Walkergate** ❹ complex, which includes the Gala Theatre, is where to find several restaurants, bars and night life.

The Garden House £ ❺ A traditional-style pub with oak beams and a fireplace, serving home-style cooking and offering a warm welcome. Just out of the centre but within walking distance. ⓐ North Road ❶ 0191 384 3460 ⓦ www.thegarden housedurham.co.uk ❶ until 21.00 daily

Bistro 21 ££ ❻ One of award-winning chef Terry Laybourne's restaurants, offering classically executed bistro dishes in this French-style establishment. Just out of the centre but within walking distance. ⓐ Aykley Heads House, Aykley Heads ❶ 0191 384 4354 ⓦ www.bistrotwentyone.co.uk ❶ 12.00–14.00, 18.00–22.00 Mon–Sat

Fallen Angel ££ ❼ Situated in the historic part of Old Elvet, here you'll find high-quality bistro-style food with locally sourced

ingredients. Rooms are also available. ➋ 34, Old Elvet
🛈 0191 384 1037 ⓦ www.fallenangelhotel.com 🕒 07.30–18.00
Sun & Mon, 09.30–23.00 Tues–Sat

Fat Buddha ££ ➒ The menu is based on Eddie Fung's fusion
restaurant of the same name in Belfast, and features a fresh
look at Chinese cuisine. Bamboo and fat Buddha statues
abound. ➋ Walkergate 🛈 0191 383 1390 ⓦ www.fatbuddha
restaurant.com/durham 🕒 12.00–14.45, 18.00–22.30 Mon–Sat,
12.00–21.30 Sun

Filini Bar & Restaurant ££ ➒ Attached to the Radisson Blu Hotel
on the river, simply cooked Italian food makes taste and flavour
the priorities. ➋ Radisson Blu Hotel, Framwellgate Waterside
🛈 0191 372 7200 ⓦ www.radissonblu.co.uk/hotel-durham/
dining 🕒 17.00–22.00 Mon–Sat

Oldfield's Eating House ££ ➓ The former HQ of the Durham
Gas Company, complete with deep red walls, solid wood
floors and large windows to create a light, airy space.
The owners believe passionately in their locally sourced
farm produce and can tell you exactly where it all comes from.
➋ 18 Claypath 🛈 0191 370 9595 ⓦ www.oldfieldsrealfood.co.uk
🕒 12.00–2.00 Mon–Sat, 12.00–21.00 Sun

Gourmet Spot £££ ⓫ Exciting fine dining for lovers of good
food, located in idyllic surroundings just out of the centre.
➋ The Avenue 🛈 0191 384 6655 ⓦ www.gourmet-spot.co.uk
🕒 17.00–late Tues–Sat

BARS & CLUBS

The Bishops Mill ⓬ Taking its name from the mill where the Freemen of Durham would go to grind their corn that used to operate on this site, this Lloyds No 1 Bar is Durham's premier late-night spot, with live DJs and dancing until late every night. ⓐ Walkergate ⓣ 0191 370 8510 ⓦ www.jdwetherspoon.co.uk ⓛ 07.00–02.00 daily

The Dun Cow ⓭ Famous small traditional pub in ancient premises on Old Elvet and home of the so-called Dun Cow Challenge – a drink from every pump on the bar in two hours! Named after the famous cow that features in the Durham legend, this pub has a good selection of real ales. ⓐ Old Elvet ⓣ 0191 386 9219 ⓛ 11.00–23.00 Mon–Sat, 12.00–23.00 Sun

Ebony ⓮ An amazing selection of champagnes and cocktails are available in this champagne bar on the Piazza level of the Walkergate Complex. ⓐ Walkergate ⓣ 0191 375 7121 ⓦ www.ebonychampagnebar.co.uk ⓛ 10.00–00.30 Mon–Wed, 10.00–01.30 Thur–Sat, 12.00–00.30 Sun

The Head of Steam ⓯ Difficult to find but well worth the effort, this is a traditional pub selling real ales and good food. Child friendly – there is a play area equipped with a climbing wall and there are colouring competitions. There's also regular live music and late nights at the weekend. ⓐ 3 Reform Place, North Road ⓣ 0191 383 2173 ⓦ www.theheadofsteam.co.uk/durham ⓛ 11.00–24.00 Mon–Thur, 11.00–02.00 Fri & Sat, 12.00–23.00 Sun

Love Shack 🔟 Enjoy your drink in a VW Caravette inside the bar and enjoy the fun and funky DJs who play here nightly. ⓐ Walkergate ⓣ 0191 384 5757 ⓦ www.loveshackdurham.com ⓛ 22.00–02.00 Wed & Thur, 20.00–02.00 Fri & Sat

The Swan and Three Cygnets 🔟 Occupying two floors and a beer garden beside Elvet Bridge, this recently refurbished traditional pub serves a wide selection of beers and wines. Frequented by locals and students alike, it also serves food. ⓐ Elvet Bridge ⓣ 0191 384 0242 ⓛ 11.00–23.00 Mon–Sat, 12.00–22.30 Sun

▶ *Nose's Point near Seaham*

OUT OF TOWN
trips

Durham Heritage Coast

Stretching from Sunderland in the north to the port of
Hartlepool in the south, the Durham Heritage Coast has been
transformed from a grim industrial landscape, with collieries
and spoil heaps, into a magnificent coastline featuring dramatic
views of undulating grassland, splendid beaches, ancient
wooded denes and yellow magnesian limestone cliffs. All this
has been achieved since the early 1990s, when the £10-million
'Turning the Tide' regeneration project began restoring
grasslands from pit heaps.

Before 'King Coal', the Durham coastline was unspoilt, with
long stretches of sand indented by the rivers Wear and Tees.
During the so-called Dark Ages, the whole of Northumbria was
in the forefront of the advance of Celtic Christendom and the
historian the Venerable Bede worked on his manuscripts at
Monkwearmouth (modern Sunderland). The Saxon church at
Seaham dates from this time.

The advent of the coal industry, which had its beginnings in
medieval times, began to change the nature of the terrain as
the mine owners sought to exploit their valuable commodity.
Gradually the coast became an industrial wasteland.

Tipping of colliery waste on to the beaches was stopped in
1993 and since then the natural action of sea has cleared much
of the spoil, uncovering the natural sandy aspect of large parts
of the coastline. Behind the beaches the grassland supports
plants and wildlife, and much of the coast has been designated
a National Nature Reserve, including several Sites of Special
Scientific Interest (SSSI).

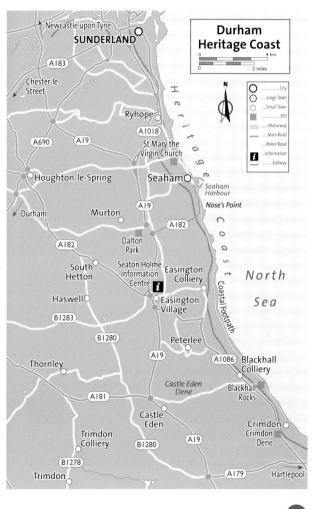

GETTING THERE

By car, take the A690 from Durham to Sunderland. At
Houghton-le-Spring, turn south on to the A19 in the direction of
Teeside and at the next junction, take the A1404 to Seaham.
There is an hourly bus service from Durham North Road Bus
Station to Seaham, which takes about an hour (🚌 Bus: 65). The
coast can be explored on foot by the well-surfaced Coastal Path
from Seaham, although appropriate footwear is advised.

SIGHTS & ATTRACTIONS

Information on the Heritage Coast can be obtained from the
Heritage Coast Information Centre at Seaton Holme in Easington
Village and tourist information centres throughout the county.

◗ *The view north along the coast from Crimdon*

⬥ *Dog-walkers on the coastal footpath*

The Durham Heritage Coastal Footpath

The Durham Heritage Coastal Footpath stretches the 18 km
(11 miles) from Seaham Hall Beach in the north to Crimdon Dene
in the south. There are several very flat, easy sections of the path,
notably from Seaham Harbour to Nose's Point and from Crimdon
Park to Crimdon Dene. It can be accessed from several places,
including Seaham, and there are car parks at several locations
along the route. The sights are listed as they appear from
north to south.

Seaham

Seaham was originally known as Seaham Harbour, the harbour
having been constructed by the 3rd Marquis of Londonderry in
1828 for the purpose of exporting coal. He later commissioned
Newcastle architect John Dobson to draw up plans for a model

town, but only North Terrace was ever built. Following the closure of all the local mines in the early 1990s, Seaham went into decline, but in recent years there has been a revival of its fortunes, due in part to the decision of the tourism authorities to create a 'lively harbour town on the Durham Heritage Coast' as part of the 'Turning the Tide' project. The town has now been transformed and the North Dock and Harbour area has undergone a £3.25-million regeneration, including a marina that complements the fine beach to the north of the town, and numerous other improvements.

Nose's Point
Nose's Point, as the name suggests, is a rocky promontory jutting out into the North Sea, and is an important conservation area. Situated just to the south of Seaham on the site of the former Dawdon Colliery and overlooking Blast Beach, views extend beyond the Heritage Coast to Tynemouth in the north and Middlesbrough in the south. The artwork, poetry and seats found along the recently landscaped cliff top, together with fantastic views, make this an ideal picnic spot. There is a car park just off the main coastal road.

Castle Eden Dene
Castle Eden Dene is a Natural England Nature Reserve and one of the very few places in England where the ancient wild woodland that used to cover much of the landscape still survives. Known for its yew trees, there are said to be 10,000 years of wild growth in the gorge. The Saxons called this Yoden or Yew dene, which eventually gave us the modern name of

Eden. Towards Blackhall Colliery, there is a splendid brick viaduct, constructed in 1905, with ten arches, each spanning 18 m (60 ft), built to carry the coastal railway. ❷ Access is from either the Coastal Path or from the A1086 just southwest of Peterlee.

Blackhall Rocks

Blackhall Rocks are just to the south of Blackhall Colliery, which, when it was sunk, was one of the most modern in England. Paradoxically, it was one of the first to shut in 1981, but not before the beach and coastline to the south had been despoiled. Nevertheless, nature has done its work and the beaches are now much cleaner and support a rich flora. Many local legends involving smugglers surround the rocks, some of which have been given nicknames reflecting their shape, such as 'Elephant Rock'.

⬥ *Seaham has been revitalised in recent times*

ⓐ Access is from either the Coastal Path or from the village of the same name via a minor road off the A1086.

Crimdon

Crimdon is located towards the southern end of the Heritage Coast and boasts a magnificent beach to complement the splendid views from the dunes both to the north and south. Just behind the beach is the beautiful Crimdon Dene, over which tower the arches of the spectacular viaduct built to carry the coastal railway. From early May, at the southern end of the Dene, you may be lucky enough to see some of the rare Little Terns that flock here from the Antarctic each summer. ⓐ Access is from either the Coastal Path or from the A1086

CULTURE

Easington Village

Easington is an ancient village dating back to the early 10th century and the name is thought to derive from the Saxon for 'Village of Esa'. Its most famous resident was the man who became England's only pope to date, in 1154, Nicholas Breakspear. The Church of St Mary on the magnificent village green is 12th century, and the rectory, now known as Seaton Holme, was built in the mid-13th century and is now an information point for the Heritage Coast. ⓐ Seaton Holme, Easington Village ⓣ 0191 527 3333 ⓦ www.durhamweb.org.uk/SeatonHolme ⓛ 08.30–17.00 Mon–Thur, 08.30–16.30 Fri

St James's Church in Castle Eden Dene

St Mary the Virgin Church

St Mary the Virgin Church at Seaham is one of the 20 oldest churches in the country and is the sole surviving building of the original village. Founded by King Athelstan in AD 930, it has a 7th-century nave and late Saxon windows, while more recent additions include an Elizabethan pulpit and stained-glass windows featuring Pre-Raphaelite designs. @ Coast Road, Seaham 🕐 0191 534 6492 🕑 14.00–16.00 Wed & Sat (May–Sept)

RETAIL THERAPY

Dalton Park A retail outlet centre located just southwest of Seaham Harbour with over 60 outlet shops offering up to 50 per cent off high-street prices on all major brands. @ Off the A19 road, Murton, County Durham 🕐 0191 526 6500 🌐 www.dalton-park.co.uk 🕑 10.00–18.00 Mon–Wed & Fri, 10.00–20.00 Thur, 09.30–18.00 Sat, 10.30–17.00 Sun

TAKING A BREAK

There is a good selection of cafés, although these are mostly in Seaham. In nearby Dalton Park there are several fast-food outlets, as well as coffee shops.

Lickety Split Creamery £ This recently opened, 1950s-style, American ice-cream parlour has occasional appearances made by 'Elvis'! Blanket hire is available if you would like to enjoy your ice cream or coffee on the grass of Terrace

Green opposite, overlooking the sea. ❸ 13 North Terrace, Seaham ❶ 0800 917 5531 Ⓦ www.lickety-split.co.uk ❶ 10.00–19.00 daily

Poppies Café Bar £ Enjoy the home-made cakes and scones baked every morning in this seafront café, popular with the locals as well as visitors to the coast. ❸ 4 South Crescent, Seaham ❶ 0191 581 7008 ❷ denise.poppies@googlemail.com ❶ 10.00–16.00 daily

AFTER DARK

Featherbed Rock Café £ Freshly prepared food and a good selection of beers and wines, and occasionally live entertainment, are available from the bar in its new venue opposite Terrace Green. ❸ 19–20 North Terrace, Seaham ❶ 0191 513 0099 Ⓦ www.featherbedrockcafe.co.uk ❶ 09.00–23.00 Sun–Thur, 09.00–24.00 Fri & Sat

Pan Din Thai Restaurant ££ This 4-star restaurant on the seafront at Seaham, above Poppies Café Bar, serves real Thai cuisine in a traditional Thai ambience enhanced by a fine selection of beers and wines. ❸ 4 South Crescent, Seaham ❶ 0191 581 2348 Ⓦ www.pandinthai.co.uk ❶ 11.30–14.30, 17.30–22.00 daily

The White Room £££ Seaham Hall's restaurant is acknowledged as the finest in County Durham and *Harden's Restaurant Guide* named it as one of the top 20 outside of London.

① Lord Byron's Walk, Seaham **☏** 0191 516 1400 **ⓦ** www.seaham-hall.co.uk **🕔** 19.00–23.00 daily

ACCOMMODATION

The Hillcarter Hotel ££ Located in the centre of Hartlepool close to the Marina, just south of the Heritage Coast, this hotel features a rooftop restaurant with amazing views. **①** Church Street, Hartlepool **☏** 0142 985 5800 **ⓦ** www.hillcarterhotel.com

Seaham Hall £££ Once the home of Lord Byron, this luxury hotel and spa, located on a cliff top on the seafront at Seaham, is one of only a few hotels outside of London to be awarded five AA red stars. **①** Lord Byron's Walk, Seaham **☏** 0191 516 1400 **ⓦ** www.seaham-hall.co.uk

⬤ *Hawthorn Viaduct, near Easington Village*

The Durham Dales

The magnificent Durham Dales are situated to the west of Durham city. Both Weardale and Teesdale are part of the North Pennines Area of Outstanding Natural Beauty (AONB), a protected area created in 1988, which was voted the fourth quietest place in Britain in 2007 by the Campaign to Protect Rural England. This area incorporates many of the most impressive landscapes in the county, including the splendid waterfalls of High Force and Cauldron Snout. Closer to Durham can be found many places of interest, including the 12th-century Auckland Castle and the unique Bowes Museum at Barnard Castle.

It's hard to believe that little over 100 years ago this region was a major centre of lead mining, smelting and quarrying. The presence of lead and other minerals in these parts has been known since ancient times and it is no accident that when the Romans drew their boundary, marked by Hadrian's Wall, it was to the north of these deposits. After the Romans left, the Celtic Britons of the area were overrun by the Saxons. They settled here only to be followed later by Vikings, who came first as raiders but eventually also stayed.

In medieval times, the region, especially Weardale, was dominated by the prince bishops, who regarded the Dale as one large hunting ground and held their so-called 'Great Chases' here. They also encouraged the development of lead mining, the proceeds of which helped to fund their lavish lifestyles. This industry was to be the mainstay of the economy of the Dales right through to the early 20th century. Limestone quarrying and cement production, together with marble quarrying in

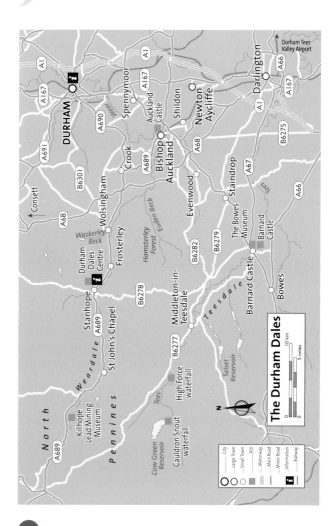

The Durham Dales

Durham Tees Valley Airport

DURHAM

Spennymoor
Auckland Castle
Shildon
Newton Aycliffe
Darlington

Crook
Bishop Auckland
Staindrop

Wolsingham
Evenwood
The Bowes Museum
Barnard Castle

Waskerley Beck
Frosterley
Hamsterley Forest
Euden beck

Durham Dales Centre

Stanhope
B6278
Middleton-in-Teesdale
Teesdale
Barnard Castle
Bowes

St John's Chapel

Selset Reservoir

North Pennines
High Force waterfall

Killhope Lead Mining Museum

Cow Green Reservoir
Cauldron Snout waterfall

N

Weardale

Consett

The Durham Dales

10 km
5 miles

City
Large Town
Small Town
POI
Motorway
Main Road
Minor Road
Information
Railway

Weardale, bolstered the economy for much of the 20th century but nowadays animal husbandry and tourism are the major industries in both Dales.

GETTING THERE

It is easier to access both Dales by car because the sights and attractions are spread out and not always easy to reach. However, there are bus services to the main towns and villages from Durham.

◆ *The River Tees at Barnard Castle*

OUT OF TOWN

Teesdale By car take the A690 east to the A1(M), head south and exit at junction 61 direction A688 Bishop Auckland and then on to Barnard Castle. From Barnard Castle the B6277 or B6278 will take you into the Upper Dale. Bus services connect Durham with Bishop Auckland  Bus: 5, 5A, 5B, 56, 56A and Bishop Auckland with Barnard Castle  Bus: 88

Weardale By car take the A690 west towards Willington and Crook. From Crook continue on the A689 to Wolsingham and the Upper Dale. By bus there are connections between Durham and Stanhope  Bus: 46A and Bishop Auckland, Wolsingham, Frosterley, Stanhope and Killhope  Bus: 101

SIGHTS & ATTRACTIONS

Barnard Castle (Teesdale)

Nicknamed 'Barney' by the locals, Barnard Castle is named after the fortress built here in 1125 by Bernard Baliol, and famous residents have included Richard III and Henry VII. This magnificent Norman structure, now in ruins, towers over the River Tees. Barnard Castle is a typical Dales town with attractive streets, old stone-built houses and a marketplace with an octagonal 18th-century building known as the Market Cross, which has been used over the years as a prison, a court, a town hall and a butter market. In the 19th-century Charles Dickens visited the town and stayed here while researching material for his novel, *Nicholas Nickleby*. Castle visit 📞 0183 363 8212 🕐 10.00–18.00 daily (Apr–Sept); 10.00–16.00 Sat & Sun (23 Oct–Dec & 2 Jan–Mar) ⓘ Admission charge

High Force waterfall (Teesdale)

High Force waterfall has one of the highest uninterrupted drops of water in England, plunging over 21 m (70 ft) into a deep pool. After heavy rain it is a splendid sight. It was formed where the Tees crosses the Whin Sill, on the same layer of rock on which the Roman wall was built, and is the subject of a famous painting by JMW Turner, who visited here in 1816. A short (very pleasant) woodland walk (about 550 m/600 yds) leads to the falls, but telephone ahead as poor weather can mean that access is closed. Note that great care should be taken at all times, especially in the immediate vicinity of the falls. ⓐ Forest-in-Teesdale ⓣ 0183 362 2209 ⓦ www.rabycastle.com ⓛ All year round, weather permitting ⓘ Admission and car park charge

⬥ High Force

Middleton-in-Teesdale (Teesdale)

Middleton is a small picturesque market town on the banks of the Tees dating back to Viking times, although it remained a very small village until the 19th century when it became a significant mining centre. The town was fortunate to be the base of the London Lead Company, owned by Quakers, which proved to be a benevolent employer unlike many others in the Dales. Nearby at Newbiggin is the oldest Methodist chapel in continuous use, since its erection in 1759.

Weardale villages

Stanhope is a historic market town with a cobbled marketplace and an industrial heritage based on lead mining and limestone quarrying. All this has gone, but a visit to the Durham Dales Centre in Castle Gardens provides local information and refreshments. The 12th-century church of St Thomas, often

🔺 *Wolsingham is one of the oldest market towns in County Durham*

known as 'the little Cathedral of the Dale', used to be known as 'the richest living in the north' due to the tithes taken from the lead miners of the area. **Frosterley**, apart from being a pretty village, is famous for a particular type of marble quarried near here. The marble, known locally as 'cockle', is formed from black carboniferous limestone speckled with the remains of plants and sea creatures and can be found in Durham Cathedral.
Wolsingham, often called the gateway to Weardale, is a small picturesque town and host to England's oldest agricultural show. Situated at the confluence of the river Wear and the Waskerley Beck, it was founded in Saxon times and is recorded in the Waskerley Domesday Book.

CULTURE

Auckland Castle (Weardale)

Auckland Castle, situated in the pleasant market town of Bishop Auckland, was established in the 12th century as a hunting lodge for the prince bishops. Since 1832, it has been the bishop's main residence. The main focus of interest in the palace is the priceless collection of Zurburán paintings. Francisco de Zurburán, a contemporary of El Greco and Velásquez, was commissioned by the Church in the mid-17th century to paint a series of works entitled *Jacob and His Twelve Sons* to promote Catholicism in Mexico. Somehow, over a hundred years later, these fell into the hands of Bishop Trevor and they have been proudly on display ever since. There are also state rooms to visit, including the original throne room and the King Charles I Dining Room. ⓐ Bishop Auckland ⓣ 0138 860 2576

ⓦ www.auckland-castle.co.uk ⏰ 14.00–17.00 Sun & Mon
(Easter Mon–Sept); 14.00–17.00 Sun, 11.00–17.00 Mon,
11.00–17.00 Wed (July & Aug) ⓘ Admission charge

The Bowes Museum (Teesdale)

A large French-style château is not what you expect to find in
rural England, but nevertheless, a short walk from the centre of
the historic market town of Barnard Castle leads you to one
such structure. Built to house the varied collections of John
Bowes and his French wife, Josephine, it was completed in 1892.
The result is a magnificent, highly ornamented and recently
renovated stone structure, with splendid gardens and parkland.
The museum's most celebrated exhibits are the musical

🔺 *The somewhat incongruous Bowes Museum*

automaton the Silver Swan, and paintings by Canaletto, El Greco and Turner, but there are also vast collections of ceramics and glass, dress and textiles and other fine art, all put together by John and Josephine, before her untimely death in 1874. In addition, there are temporary exhibitions featuring works by artists such as Monet, Toulouse-Lautrec and JMW Turner. ⓐ Barnard Castle ⓣ 0183 369 0606 ⓦ www.thebowes museum.org.uk ⓣ 10.00–17.00 daily; closed 25 & 26 Dec, 1 Jan ⓘ Admission charge

Killhope Lead Mining Museum (Teesdale)

Located in Upper Weardale, this museum gives an excellent insight into the daily life of the lead miners of the 19th century. It includes working waterwheels, a 'mineshop' where the miners lived, a mine tour and various 'hands-on' experiences. ⓐ Near Cowshill, Upper Weardale ⓣ 0138 853 7505 ⓦ www.killhope. org.uk ⓣ 10.30–17.00 daily (Apr–Oct) ⓘ Admission charge

RETAIL THERAPY

Shopping in the Dales tends to be concentrated in Barnard Castle, with a few shops only in the relatively small Dales towns.

Boyes Set over three levels in Barnard Castle's main street, this always-busy Aladdin's cave of a shop offers everything from toys and clothes through to fishing equipment and kitchenware. ⓐ 28/32 Horse Market, Barnard Castle ⓣ 0183 363 7233 ⓦ www.boyes.co.uk/stores/barnard_store.html ⓣ 09.00–17.30 Mon–Sat, 10.30–16.30 Sun

Gemcraft This jewellery shop in the Durham Dales Centre specialises in Weardale minerals, Frosterley marble and semi-precious gemstone jewellery. There's also a children's section. ⓐ Durham Dales Centre, Stanhope ☎ 0138 852 6233 🌐 www.gemsandfossils.com 🕙 10.00–17.00 daily (Apr–Oct); 10.00–16.00 daily (Nov–Mar)

Grants Contemporary Art Contemporary art by Stephanie Grant (a locally renowned artist and art dealer) can be found in this gallery near to The Bowes Museum in the centre of Barnard Castle ⓐ 26, Newgate, Barnard Castle ☎ 0183 369 5700 🌐 www.grantscontemporaryart.co.uk 🕙 11.00–13.00, 14.00–17.00 Tues–Sun (May–Sept); 11.00–13.00, 14.00–17.00 Tues–Sat (Oct–Apr)

Mission Hall Antiques Centre The North East's newest antiques centre boasts five antique shops with more than 30 cabinets with everything from Worcester and Beswick to 20th-century work, plus a variety of other interesting items including books, medals and vintage clothing. ⓐ 51 The Bank, Barnard Castle ☎ 0183 363 1101 🌐 www.missionhall antiquescentre.co.uk 🕙 Mon–Sat 10.00–17.00, Sun 13.30–17.00

TAKING A BREAK

There is a good selection of places to have morning coffee, lunch or afternoon tea scattered throughout the Dales, both at the visitor attractions and in the towns. There are also several excellent restaurants throughout the region.

Café Bowes £ Recently refurbished, this acclaimed café offers high-quality fare, much of it locally sourced, without having to pay to enter the museum. ⓐ Bowes Museum ⓣ 0183 369 0606 ⓦ www.thebowesmuseum.org.uk ⓛ 10.00–16.30 daily

Durham Dales Centre Tea Room £ After browsing through the information provided on the Dales, enjoy some morning coffee or a home-baked afternoon tea in the courtyard of the Dales Centre. ⓐ Durham Dales Centre, Stanhope ⓣ 0138 852 7650 ⓦ www.durhamdalescentre.co.uk ⓛ 10.00–17.00 daily (Apr–Oct); 10.00–16.00 daily (Nov–Mar)

Killhope Café £ Part of the Lead Mining Museum, and now an attraction itself, the café serves home-made soups and puddings made from organic and/or locally sourced ingredients. ⓐ Killhope Lead Mining Museum, Cowshill ⓣ 0138 853 7505 ⓦ www.killhope.org.uk ⓛ 10.30–17.00 daily (Apr–Oct)

AFTER DARK

Spice Island Restaurant £ Experience the cuisine of the whole Indian subcontinent in the Market Place at Barnard Castle, at this tranquil, contemporary and informal restaurant. ⓐ 9 Market Place, Barnard Castle ⓣ 0183 363 0575 ⓦ www.spice islandrestaurant.co.uk ⓛ 17.30–23.00 daily

The Forresters Restaurant ££ In the centre of Middleton-in-Teesdale and picturesquely located at the confluence of the Tees

and the Hudeshope Beck, the Forresters was re-opened recently by French chef Fabien Hombourger. ⓐ 52/53 Market Place, Middleton-in-Teesdale ⓣ 0183 364 1435 ⓦ www.forresters middleton.co.uk ⓛ 11.00–22.00 daily

The Rose & Crown ££ An 18th-century coaching inn located on the green of one of the region's prettiest villages, Romaldkirk. Voted in 2006 Michelin Pub of the Year, the restaurant boasts the TasteDurham Highest Quality Award. ⓐ Romaldkirk, Barnard Castle ⓣ 0183 365 0213 ⓦ www.rose-and-crown.co.uk ⓛ 12.00–13.30, 19.30–21.00 daily

The Teesdale Hotel ££ In the heart of the Dales, this restaurant in the lovely village of Middleton-in-Teesdale has timeless character and an excellent reputation for its high-quality cuisine. ⓐ Market Place, Middleton-in-Teesdale ⓣ 0183 364 0264 ⓦ www.teesdalehotel.co.uk ⓛ 12.00–14.30, 19.00–20.45 daily

ACCOMMODATION

The Manor House Hotel ££ This Jacobean Grade I-listed building situated near the picturesque village green at West Auckland offers 35 comfortably furnished rooms, some with four-poster beds. ⓐ West Auckland ⓣ 0138 883 4834 ⓦ www.manorhouse hotel.net

● *Durham is served by three Park and Ride sites*

PRACTICAL
information

Directory

GETTING THERE

Durham can be reached either from Durham Tees Valley or Newcastle International Airports, the latter of which is used by many of the major airlines, including BA and easyJet. There are regular flights to Newcastle from London (Stansted and Heathrow), Belfast and Bristol; and to Durham from Dublin, Southampton and Aberdeen.

British Airways Ⓦ www.britishairways.com
easyJet Ⓦ www.easyjet.com
Aer Lingus Ⓦ www.aerlingus.com
Eastern Airways Ⓦ www.easternairways.com

Many people are aware that air travel emits CO_2, which contributes to climate change. You may be interested in the possibility of lessening the environmental impact of your flight through the charity **Climate Care** (Ⓦ www.jpmorgan climatecare.com), which offsets your CO_2 by funding environmental projects around the world.

By train

If you are travelling to Durham from London or the southeast of England, trains from King's Cross usually take just under three hours. At peak times, there are trains every 5 to 30 minutes. From Manchester, it takes about 2 hours 20 minutes, while from Edinburgh the journey time is less than 2 hours. Fares are variable and depend on how far ahead you book.

East Coast Trains Ⓦ www.eastcoast.co.uk
Virgin Trains Ⓦ www.virgintrains.co.uk
thetrainline Ⓦ www.thetrainline.com

By coach

The coach takes longer than the train – in fact, about twice as long on average – but prices are much lower. National Express coaches run five services per day to Durham North Road Bus Station from London, which take 6 to 7 hours 30 minutes. There are six services per day from Manchester and three services per day from Edinburgh Ⓦ www.nationalexpress.com

By car

Although the car will be of little use for exploring Durham city, for many UK visitors it may be the most convenient way of reaching the city, especially if you live some distance from London or the other major conurbations. Routes are quite straightforward and from many parts of the country it is possible to use the motorway network for large sections of the journey.

HEALTH, SAFETY & CRIME

The only Accident and Emergency department in the city is based at the University Hospital of North Durham, in North Road about 1.5 km (1 mile) northwest of the Market Place. There is currently no minor injuries unit or walk-in centre in Durham. As mentioned in the 'On Arrival' section of this guide, crime is less of a problem in Durham than in most other UK cities. The police station is situated on New Elvet. ☎ 0345 606 0365 ⏱ 08.00–19.00 Mon–Fri, 09.00–17.00 Sat & Sun

TOILETS

There are public toilets in the Gates Shopping Centre and the Indoor Market, on Palace Green, in the cathedral cloisters and in North Road beside the road up to the railway station.

CHILDREN

Durham is a child-friendly city and well-behaved children are welcome in most establishments. All of the museums have exhibits aimed specifically at younger age groups. Children love to be taken on rowing boats, which can be hired from Brown's Boathouse beside Elvet Bridge, and Durham City Pool (closed Sun) is always a great source of fun for the whole family.

TRAVELLERS WITH DISABILITIES

Travellers with disabilities are well catered for in Durham. The Prince Bishops Shopping Centre offers a Shopmobility scheme with special parking arrangements on Level 1 of its multi-storey car park. The scheme also provides scooters and wheelchairs for an hourly rate, and long-term loans up to one week can be arranged (☏ 0191 386 8556 ⏱ Tues–Sat). The Gates Shopping Centre has disabled spaces on Level 3 of its car park and Walkergate has spaces also. All surface car parks have disabled spaces and blue badge holders can park for unlimited periods in the off-street parking spaces and permit-holder areas. Some historic buildings might present a problem since they cannot always be adapted. The cathedral authorities, however, provide ramps and have recently acquired a 'stairclimber', although some areas, such as the Shrine of St Cuthbert, have no disabled access or are difficult to reach. Help is provided for those with impaired vision and hearing (🕿 0191 386 4267). Most other attractions or facilities offer some disabled access but it is advisable to telephone first to discuss individual requirements.

A useful source of general information and advice on disability issues is RADAR 🄰 12 City Forum, 250 City Road, London EC1V 8AF 🕿 0207 250 3222 🌐 www.radar.org.uk

FURTHER INFORMATION

There is one tourist information centre in Durham based in Millennium Square, where you can obtain a map of the city and other useful information free of charge.

Durham Tourist Information Centre 🄰 Millennium Square
🕿 0191 384 3720 🌐 www.thisisdurham.com 🕒 09.30–17.30 Mon–Fri, 09.00–17.30 Sat

Peterlee Tourist Information Centre (for Durham Heritage Coast) 🄰 Upper Yoden Way, Peterlee 🕿 0191 586 4450
🕒 09.00–17.00 Mon–Thur, 09.00–16.30 Fri, 09.00–14.00 Sat

Useful websites include:
🌐 www.englandsnortheast.co.uk
🌐 www.durhamheritagecoast.org
🌐 www.durhamdales.co.uk
🌐 http://durham.pindar.com (Durham County Interactive Transport Mapping)

A1 2/13 BB/2/13

ACKNOWLEDGEMENTS

The photographs in this book were taken by Paul Walters for Thomas Cook Publishing, to whom the copyright belongs.

Project editor: Tom Lee
Copy editor: Emma Haigh
Layout: Donna Pedley
Proofreaders: Penny Isaac & Richard Gilbert
Indexer: Penelope Kent

AUTHOR BIOGRAPHY

Paul Shawcross has been a travel journalist for over twenty years, writing guidebooks and magazine articles that normally feature the sunnier climes of southern Europe. However, he does take great pleasure in penning pieces about his native northeast when the opportunity arises.

Send your thoughts to
books@thomascook.com

- Found a great bar, club, shop or must-see sight that we don't feature?
- Like to tip us off about any information tha eds a little updating?
- Want to tell us what you love about this ha little guidebook and more importantly how we can make it even handier?

Then here's your chance to tell all! Send us ideas, discoveries and recommendations today and then look out for your valuable input in the next edition of this title.

Email the above address (stating the title) or write to:
pocket guides Series Editor, Thomas Cook Publishing, PO Box 227, Coningsby Road, Peterborough PE3 8SB, UK.